TOOLS FOR TEACHERS

- **ATOS:** 0.8
- **LEXILE:** 50L
- **CURRICULUM CONNECTIONS:** patterns, sorting
- **WORD COUNT:** 57

Skills to Teach

- **HIGH-FREQUENCY WORDS:** a, at, has, is, look, the, what
- **CONTENT WORDS:** balls, boat, chairs, pattern, shells, shoes, towels
- **PUNCTUATION:** periods, question marks, exclamation point
- **WORD STUDY:** double consonants (*balls*, *pattern*, *shells*); long /o/, spelled oa (*boat*); long /u/, spelled oe (*shoes*); dipthong /ou/, spelled ow (*towels*)
- **TEXT TYPE:** factual description

Before Reading Activities

- Read the title and give a simple statement of the main idea.
- Have students "walk" though the book and talk about what they see in the pictures.
- Introduce new vocabulary by having students predict the first letter and locate the word in the text.
- Discuss any unfamiliar concepts that are in the text.

After Reading Activities

Write the book's language pattern in two columns on the board: "Look at the _____." and "What is the pattern?" Encourage children to look around the room and identify things that have patterns. Write their answers under the first column. Then identify and discuss the different kinds of patterns they see (stripes, spots, etc.), and write them down under the second column.

Tadpole Books are published by Jump!, 5357 Penn Avenue South, Minneapolis, MN 55419, www.jumplibrary.com

Copyright ©2018 Jump. International copyright reserved in all countries. No part of this book may be reproduced in any form without written permission from the publisher.

Editor: Jenny Fretland VanVoorst **Designer:** Anna Peterson

Photo Credits: Getty: Greg Ceo, 2–3; KidStock, 14–15. iStock: andrewburgess, 10–11. Shutterstock: TerraceStudio, cover; Brooke Becker, 1; Pavle-Marjanovic, 4–5; Fotoluminate LLC, 6–7; Lorant Matyas, 8–9; holbox, 12–13.

Library of Congress Cataloging-in-Publication Data
Names: Mayerling, Tim, author.
Title: Patterns in summer / by Tim Mayerling.
Description: Minneapolis, Minnesota: Jump!, Inc., 2017. | Series: Patterns in the seasons | Audience: Ages 3–6. | Includes index. | Description based on print version record and CIP data provided by publisher; resource not viewed.
Identifiers: LCCN 2016058412 (print) | LCCN 2017011244 (ebook) | ISBN 9781624966057 (ebook) | ISBN 9781620317587 (hardcover: alk. paper) | ISBN 9781620317785 (pbk.)
Subjects: LCSH: Pattern perception—Juvenile literature. | Summer—Juvenile literature.
Classification: LCC BF294 (ebook) | LCC BF294 .M388 2017 (print) | DDC 152.14/23—dc23
LC record available at https://lccn.loc.gov/2016058412

PATTERNS IN THE SEASONS

PATTERNS IN SUMMER

by Tim Mayerling

TABLE OF CONTENTS

tadpole
books

PATTERNS IN SUMMER

Look at the towels.

towel

What is the pattern?

Look at the balls.

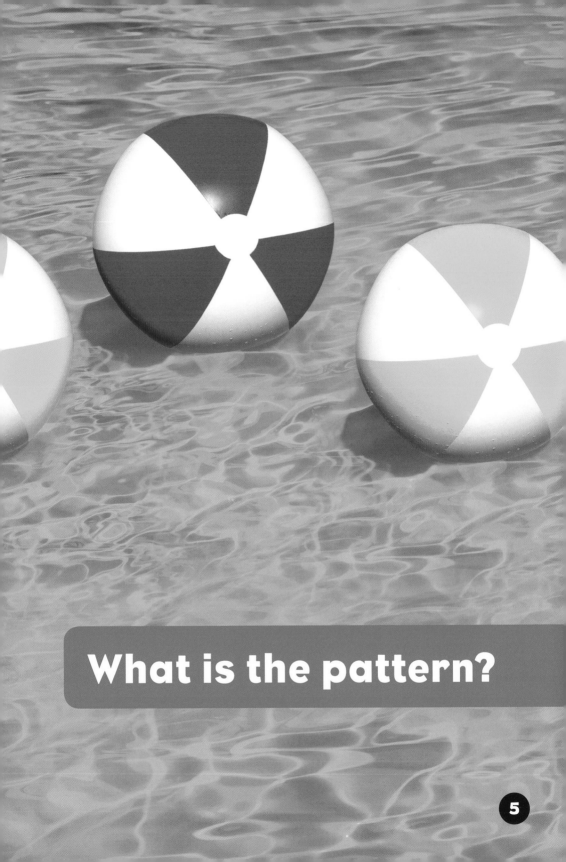

What is the pattern?

Look at the chairs.

What is the pattern?

Look at the shells.

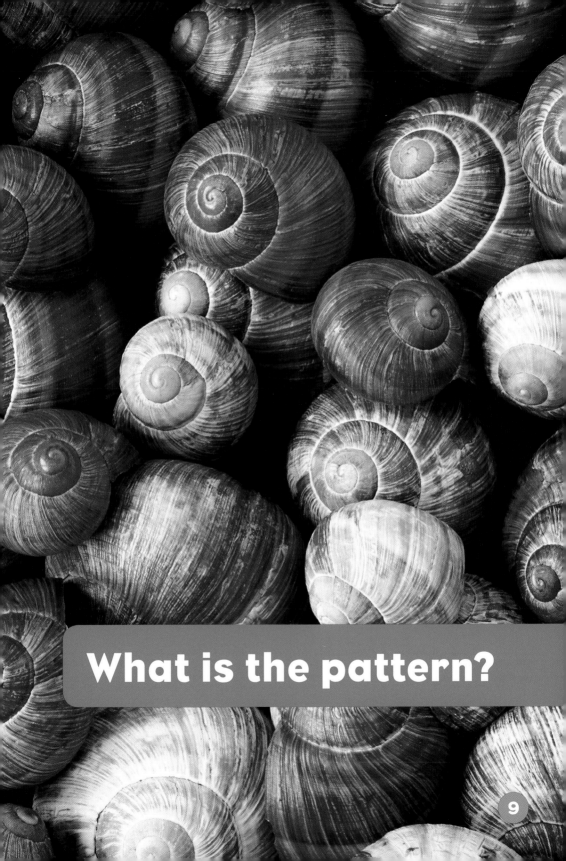

What is the pattern?

Look at the shoes.

What is the pattern?

Look at the boat.

What is the pattern?

Look!

What else has a pattern?

15

WORDS TO KNOW

balls

boat

chairs

shells

shoes

towels

INDEX

16